The Greenleaf Guide to
Famous Men of the
Renaissance
& Reformation

by Cynthia A. Shearer
& Robert G. Shearer

Greenleaf Press
Lebanon, Tennessee

Published by

Greenleaf Books, LLC

First Edition, January 1998
Third Printing, May 2001

Internet: *www.greenleafpress.com*
3761 Highway 109 N., Unit D
Lebanon, TN 37087
615-449-1617

History for the thoughtful child

Introduction

When you want to build something, a hammer is a very useful thing to have. But if someone picks up your hammer and starts beating you over the head with it, the hammer is no longer a tool — it's a murder weapon. So it is with textbooks and study guides. Used correctly, they are useful tools — but don't let anyone use them as a weapon to beat you up with a rigid list of "how you should be doing it..." Like all Greenleaf Guides, this book is intended to be used as a tool, a possible model for you to use and adapt as you see fit. You will know what suggestions will work best for the students you teach, and you should feel free to make the course fit your family's needs.

The Study Guide is designed to be used with the **Famous Men of the Renaissance and Reformation** text. It also makes suggestions for other readings from various fiction and non-fiction sources and provides lists of vocabulary and a list of the important places and people mentioned in each chapter. We have also included suggested discussion questions for each chapter. Some of them may be useful starting points for written assignments, but for the most part, they are intended merely as a guide to the teacher — as a starting point for discussion rather than "questions found at the end of the chapter, to be answered by the students by copying passages from the text." If your high school experience was anything like ours, you probably have the same negative reaction to that style of teaching that we do.

A word about discussion: in our family study we have begun using narration as a beginning point for our discussions. We highly recommend the practice to you. It is one of the basic building blocks of the Charlotte Mason approach. Here is the way she describes it:

> "As knowledge is not assimilated until it is reproduced, children should "tell back" after a single reading or hearing: or should write on some part of what they have read. A single reading is insisted on, because children have naturally great power of attention; but this force is dissipated by the re-reading of passages, and also, by questioning, summarizing , and the like."
>
> — **A Philosophy of Education**, Introduction.

In practice, here is how narration works. We read (or they read) the passage once and then they tell it back to us in their own words. As they are narrating, we try not to comment — unless there is some gross misunderstanding. Any background material — such as map skills, or definitions of words expected to be problematic — should be given before the reading so that they will be able to read with understanding the first time through. When we first asked them to tell us what they had just read, there were lots of long empty pauses, and looks that begged for rescue. But each week has brought marked improvement. The reason that Miss Mason says not to ask questions as they go along, is that the interruptions interfere with their own internal "ordering" of the material. If they know you will be asking them the questions, they will wait for you to tell them what they need to remember. If left alone, they have to ask themselves the questions, and learn to identify significant details and events. I have found that by beginning our discussion with narration, we take care of the more obvious observation questions that can become so stilted and tedious. Then we can concentrate on the questions that force the child to interpret and apply his own prior stores of knowledge to the new material — evaluating and criticizing. In this setting, the discussion questions merely suggest primary themes, issues, or points of view that are central to the chapter and probably should be dealt with in some fashion. Please resist the temptation to approach the discussion questions as if they were a catechism.

A Note on multi-level teaching:

If you are using this material for older students, eighth grade and up, you may find that your students can incorporate high school level literature selections into their study. The older high school students can be reading **The Prince**, More's **Utopia**, or selections by Luther & Calvin (or perhaps even selections from **The Norton Anthology of Literature**) while the younger students are reading selections from the children's fiction set in the Renaissance and Reformation.

A Note on testing:

When we think of testing, we usually think of exams — essay questions, true/false, multiple choice. There is a place for traditional testing both in and out of conventional classroom settings, but don't overlook the other options. If after reading a story, or listening to you read it aloud, the child is able to tell you the story in his own words — you can know that he understands it. That's really the reason for testing... to make sure your student understands the material.

Another means by which you can evaluate a student's understanding of a selection is through oral discussion. As stated earlier, the "For Discussion" questions provided with each chapter are intended to be suggestions — questions you might ask. Often, as you discuss the reading, you will naturally cover the material without sticking to a rigid "question/answer" format. Treasure those times! Sometimes you will need to draw your students along point by point. Sometimes you will need to ask questions different from those suggested. By all means, do.

Written assignments also help evaluate understanding. Some "For Discussion" questions will work particularly well as essay topics. Occasionally have your students retell the story by presenting it as a news story, short story, play, etc.

For High School Students:

Although testing is less significant in most home school settings than in traditional classrooms, test taking might still be a valuable exercise for your student(s). While testing should never replace or distract from meaningful discussion between teacher and student, older students especially need to develop their test taking skills. Most importantly, students should be able to write a strong short essay.

The length of the short essay will vary according to its type. An exam essay question can often be satisfactorily answered in one or two paragraphs. Often your students will be asked to write a longer five paragraph essay. Most likely, your student(s) will respond less than graciously to your efforts to make them competent in this form, but one day they will either rise up and call you blessed or kick themselves repeatedly for not taking you more seriously. This kind of essay is a staple of college writing assignments.

In the five paragraph essay the first paragraph introduces the essay, introducing the key points to be developed, and states the thesis of the essay (the dreaded thesis statement). Paragraphs two, three and four develop those key points raised in the introduction. Paragraph two should develop the first of those points. Paragraph three should develop the second of those points. Paragraph four should develop the third of those points. The final paragraph should summarize and tie everything together in a strong close. For more information about this type of essay, refer to a good English composition handbook.

The older the student, the more frequent I would make the writing assignments. After they have written, do not apologize for making them revise and revise and revise again. This kind of learning is just plain hard work. Remind them that God will reward the student who has a teachable spirit. (We won't talk about what teachers long to do to those students who lack this virtuous trait...).

Suggestions for Teacher Preparation:

1. Familiarize yourself with the chronology of the period, so that you have a sense of where you are going to begin and end. This will also briefly introduce you to the names of some of the people you will be reading about.

2. Read through the study guide's lessons and the assignments before you begin teaching them. Decide which activities you will do with which children, and which additional readings you will assign. Most of the books suggested in the guide make excellent family read aloud choices.

Books Used in This Study:

This study guide makes use of the following books — as of this writing all are in print. As in other guides, occasional references are made to back issues of National Geographic Magazine, and other videos. Public Libraries and used books stores may also have books that you may find useful. One of the most disheartening things about the book business is that many excellent works of historical fiction written for children go out of print every year. They come into print in hardback, do not sell well enough to warrant reprinting in more affordable paperback editions and are thus discontinued. Keep your eyes open and you will probably stumble onto some real treasures.

Primary Texts:

Famous Men of the Renaissance and Reformation, Robert G. Shearer, Greenleaf Press, 1996

The Italian Renaissance, Living History Series, John Clare, editor, H25
Harcourt Brace, 1995

Giotto and Medieval Painting, Lucia Corrain, Peter Bedrick Books, 1996 *A 759.5*

Leonardo Da Vinci: Artist, Inventor and Scientist of the Renaissance, Francesca *A709.2 / J709.2*
Romei, Peter Bedrick Books, 1997

The Protestant Reformation: Major Documents, edited by Lewis W. Spitz, *Library*
Concordia Publishing, 1966

Supplemental Texts:

Both the Renaissance and the Reformation are incredibly rich periods, and one that seems to stir our imaginations. We believe use of the five primary texts listed above will provide you with a thorough study of the period, however, we also recommend that you add some of the following books to your study. The first six are included in ***The Greenleaf Deluxe Study Package for the Renaissance and Reformation***.

The Beggar's Bible, Louise Vernon, Herald Press (about Wyclif)

The Man Who Laid the Egg, Louise Vernon, Greenleaf Press (about Erasmus)

Thunderstorm in Church, Louise Vernon, Greenleaf Press (about Luther)

The Bible Smuggler, Louise Vernon, Herald Press (about Tyndale)

Night Preacher, Louise Vernon, Herald Press (about Menno Simons)

The Secret Church, Louise Vernon, Herald Press (about the Swiss Anabaptists)

The Prince: A New Translation, Niccolo Machiavelli, Penguin, 1996

Utopia, Sir Thomas More, Penguin, 1985

**On Fire for Christ: Stories of the Anabaptist Martyrs retold from the Martyrs'
    Mirror**, Dave and Netta Jackson, Herald Press

Getting to Know the World's Great Artists series, by Mike Venezia
    titles on Botticelli, Da Vinci, & Michelangelo

Leonardo Da Vinci, by Diane Stanley, Simon & Schuster, 1996

Michelangelo: Master of the Italian Renaissance, Gabriella di Cagno,
    Peter Bedrick Books, 1996

There are many more. Many of these books are available directly from Greenleaf Press.
Write or call for a free catalog:

Greenleaf Press
3761 Highway 109 N., Unit D
Lebanon, TN 37087

Phone: 1-800-311-1508

FAX: 615-449-4018

Email: greenleafp@aol.com

Web Address: http://www.greenleafpress.com

Note: If you have a first edition copy of **Famous Men of the Renaissance and Reformation**, the
    page numbers referenced for some chapters will be slightly different in this guide. In the
    second and later editions, we moved the chapter on Dürer from the Renaissance to the
    Reformation, between the chapters on Charles V and Zwingli. Dürer was a master of the style
    of the Italian Renaissance, but his sympathies were clearly with the Reformation.

An Overview of Renaissance Geography

All but one of the fourteen "Famous Men" of the Renaissance are Italian. To understand the events of their lives the student needs to know a few of the details of European geography beyond just the location of Italy. In 1300 there was no independent nation of Italy. Southern Italy was a separate kingdom and the cities of Northern Italy were largely independent. Although they were nominally a part of the Holy Roman Empire, they had successfully rebelled and defeated Emperor Frederick Barbarossa in the 12th century.

For a larger view of Europe, including Italy, see the maps included with the *Overview of Reformation Geography* on page 33. There is also a very good map of Europe in 1527 on the inside front flyleaf of **The Italian Renaissance** in the *Living History* series.

The best way to learn these basic geographic features is for students to complete their own map (you may photocopy as many copies of the blank map on the next page as you need). They should be able to locate and label Venice, Milan, Florence, Rome, and Naples as well as Po River, the Arno River, and the Tiber River. They should also be able to correctly locate the Appennine Mountains and to identify the islands of Sicily, Corsica & Sardenia.

After students have completed their own maps, you can test them on their knowledge by giving them a fresh blank map and asking them to label the important political and geographic features from memory.

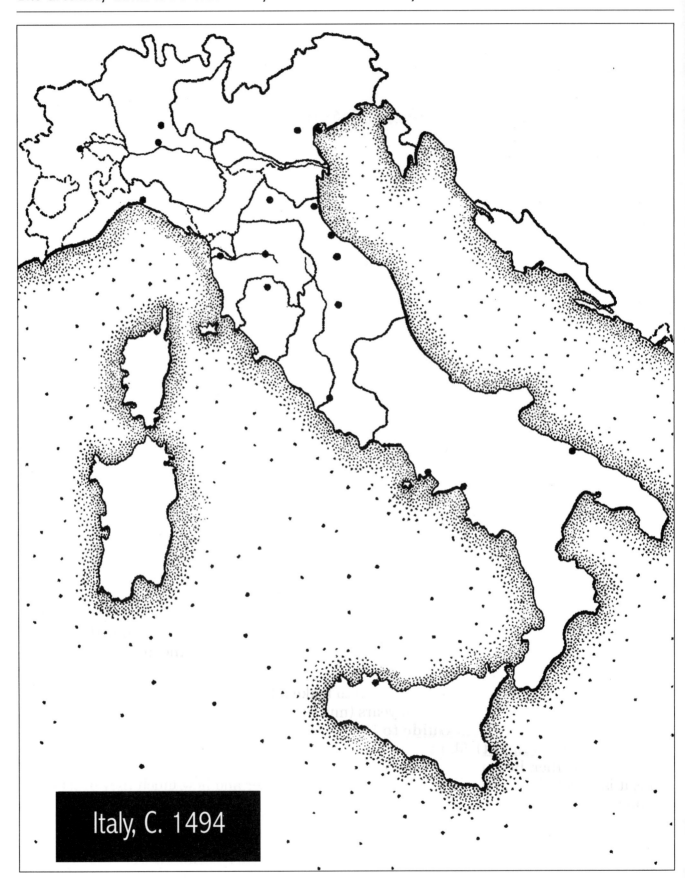

Italy, C. 1494

Introduction

Resources:

Famous Men of the Renaissance & Reformation, page 1

People and Places:

Aristotle   Plato   Cicero

Vocabulary:

rhetoric   logic   humanist
ornate   feudal kingdom

For Discussion:

In preparation for your study of the Renaissance and the Reformation periods, take a little time to review your history studies so far. Much of what you will read about in the **Famous Men of the Renaissance & Reformation** concerns the efforts to recover the knowledge of the classical world (specifically the languages) that had been lost or obscured during the Middle Ages. A review of Greek and Roman history will be especially useful, as will an overview of the impact of the Middle Ages on European civilization. For each of the three time periods, make sure your students know the following basic facts:

1. How did geography influence the history of the region (make sure your students can find the important rivers, mountains, cities and countries of Europe on a map)?

2. What issues most concerned this culture? What things did they value, honor, fight for or fight against? Who were their major enemies and allies?

3. What were the major accomplishments of their civilization? What factors contributed to the fall of this nation?

4. What were the dominant religious beliefs of the culture? Did those beliefs change over time? How and why?

5. You might want to discuss briefly with your students the definition of both logic and rhetoric. Logic is a set of rules for reasoning. Rhetoric is the art of speaking or writing persuasively.

Before you begin your study, it is helpful to make a timeline chart. The period of time covered in this book is only about 350 years (much shorter than any of the earlier *Famous Men* books or **The Greenleaf Guide to Old Testament History** or **The Greenleaf Guide to Ancient Egypt**). Many of the figures that you will study are actually contemporaries of each other. Because the chapters usually cover only one or two major figures at a time, it is easy to lose sight of how closely they fall together and how much they overlap. So, on a sheet of paper, mark off 30 vertical lines. You can use a sheet of grid-lined paper or even notebook paper, turned sideways. Make each line represent ten years. Using the birth and death dates of each figure make a bar graph, making the bar (or horizontal line) span the period of time each figure lived. Notice which figures are contemporaries.

Chapter 1
Petrarch
1304-1374

Resources:

Famous Men of the Renaissance & Reformation, pages 3-7

The Italian Renaissance, page 6-9, "A Time of Change" & "The Humanists"

People and Places:

Dante	Basel	Florence, Italy
Montpellier, France	Bologna, Italy	Avignon, France
Padua, Italy	The Iliad and The Odyssey	

Vocabulary:

exile	disenchanted	relent, relented
prestigious	poet laureate	disillusioned

For Discussion:

1. Describe Petrarch's family background. How did his father's occupation affect the family's life?

2. Describe Petrarch's schooling. What kind of education did his father choose for him?

3. How did Petrarch feel about studying law? What would he have preferred to be studying?

4. Who was Laura? Describe Petrarch's relationship with her. How well did he know her? How did she affect his life?

5. Describe Petrarch's relationship with his brother. Over time, how did it change?

6. What was Petrarch's attitude toward classical languages and civilizations? Describe his goals and accomplishments. What were the results of his study and mastery of classical Latin?

7. Petrarch's love of Latin led him to develop an interest in the writers of ancient Greece. Why was he never able to enjoy reading them?

8. What do you think of Petrarch's letter to posterity? His letter to Augustine? If you were going to write a letter to some historical figure, who would you choose? Explain the reasons for your choice. What would you say? (Perhaps someone will ask you to write the letter now... One day you will thank them for it...)

On **Sonnets**:

a) A petrarchan sonnet is exactly 14 lines long. These 14 lines are divided into two stanzas. The first stanza is 8 lines long, the second is 6 lines. Very often, the first 8 lines (or the octave) will present the problem, which is then resolved in the last six lines.

b) The rhyme scheme for the octave typically follows this pattern: ABBA CDDC. The last six lines typically follow this pattern: EFGEFG

c) Each line is written in a consistent rhythmic pattern known as *iambic pentameter*.

d) *Iambic* means that the syllables in each line alternate between unstressed and stressed syllables:
"Life HUR-ries ON a FRAN-tic REF-u-GEE"

e) *Pentameter* means that each line has five poetic feet (penta=five), or 10 syllables (since each foot has two syllables).

The Shakespearean Sonnet is made up of a single 14 line stanza that ends in a rhyming couplet, typically there is greater variety in the rhyme scheme.

Chapter 2
Giotto
1267-1336

Resources:

Famous Men of the Renaissance & Reformation, pages 9-12

The Italian Renaissance, "A Painter at Work," pages 20-21

Giotto and Medieval Art, by Lucia Corrain

Vocabulary:

vivid   execute (as in *execute several paintings*)
commission   arresting (as in *his style was vivid and arresting*)
emissary   fresco
prominent   successor
prestigious   tenure
resound   ready (as in *his ready hand*)
cite

People and Places:

Italy   Assisi
Naples   Rimini
Arezzo   Padua
Giotto (pronounced Jot'-oh)   Cimabue (pronounced Chim'-e-boo'-a)
St. Francis   the Medici (pronounced Med'-e-chee)

Background information:

As you will see as you read through this section of the study guide, you could easily spend more than one class session on this chapter. I would recommend devoting at least a week to Giotto.

There are several different ways you might use the two resources for this chapter. You might read through the entire chapter on Giotto in the **Famous Men** book and then go through **Giotto and Medieval Art**, reviewing the account of his life as appropriate. Or you could use the two books simultaneously, using **Giotto and Medieval Art** to provide background information and then add more details about the different stages of Giotto's life as told in the **Famous Men** chapter. Either approach is valid, but one is likely to feel more natural to you than the other. Follow your instincts.

The following is a short summary of the material covered in each of the two-page spreads in **Giotto and Medieval Art** with some suggestions on how each spread relates to the information in the chapter in the **Famous Men** book.

"*Contemporaries,*" pages 4-5, introduces many of the people and groups that Giotto encountered, worked with, and worked for.

"*Religious Art in the Middle Ages,*" page 6-7 and "*Churches and Cathedrals,*" pages 8-9 describe the styles of art commonly created during this period and how the various types of art were used in the decoration of cathedrals.

"*Sculpture Before the Time of Giotto,*" pages 10-11. Unless a student is familiar with sculpture and painting before Giotto, it is a little hard to appreciate his significance. These two pages attempt to provide some of that background. "*Giotto's Originality,*" page 50-51, discusses the changes Giotto brought to painting.

At this point, it would be appropriate to read the first page of the Giotto chapter (page 9) in the **Famous Men** book.

Read "*Florence in the 13th Century,*" pages 12-13 for a description of life in the famous Italian city. There is an excellent map of Florence and the surrounding region.

The four spreads from pages 14-21 provide more information concerning Cimabue (pronounced Chim'-e-boo'-a), typical artists' workshops, just what it means to paint on panels, and other general background information about drawing and painting.

At this point, read page 10 of the Giotto chapter in the **Famous Men** book. As the **Famous Men** text mentions the different places to which Giotto traveled, read pages 26-27 for insight into what was involved.

Giotto was known for his ability to paint realistically. "*Real Life,*" on pages 32-33 explains how this differed from previous styles of painting. "*Frescoes,*" on pages 34-35 further describes the details of this kind of painting.

"*The Churches at Assisi,*" on pages 28-29 and "*The Franciscans,*" on pages 30-31 tell more about the order that commissioned the paintings on the life of St. Francis. Pages 36-41 show how Giotto painted "*The Story of St. Francis.*"

At this point, read the third paragraph on page 10 of the Giotto chapter in the **Famous Men** book.

"*Jubilee Year,*" & "*Roman Mosaic Work,*" pages 42-45 tell more about Giotto's work in Rome.

At this point, read the first paragraph on page 11 of the Giotto chapter in the **Famous Men** book.

"*The Scrovegni Chapel, Padua,*" pages 48-49, and "*Giotto's Originality,*" pages 50-51 give details of the work which Giotto completed in Padua, after he left Rome, but before he returned to Florence.

At this point, read the rest of page 11 of the Giotto chapter in the **Famous Men** book.

"*In Santa Croce,*" pages 52-53 depicts some of the work done after Giotto returned to Florence, and "*Giotto as Architect,*" tells more about the building of the bell tower described in the Famous Men text.

Pages 56-61 tell more about the ways in which Giotto's work influenced other painters.

Finally, on page 62, there is a list of places where you can see Giotto's work today, including a number of museums in the United States.

For Discussion:

1. Describe Giotto's family's background. How did their lifestyle make it possible for Giotto to develop his artistic abilities?

2. Tell about Giotto's encounter with Cimabue. What changes did the meeting bring for Giotto? What kind of pupil was Giotto? What kind of person does he seem to have been?

3. What types of commissions did Giotto receive after leaving Cimabue's workshop?

4. How did the Franciscans hear about Giotto? What did they want him to do for them?

5. How did Giotto win the Pope's commission? Try to draw a perfect circle yourself with a single stroke on a sheet of paper. How close can you come? How difficult or "simple" is this task?

6. If you are using David Quine's *Cornerstone Curriculum, Adventures in Art* materials, you will find a piece by Cimabue in "Gallery I," and a piece by Giotto in "Gallery II."

7. With any of the paintings you study, you might try variations on this approach:

   • Choose a representative painting for the artist you are studying.

   • Have your students look at it carefully. Then have them tell you what details they notice. Who or what is the painting about? Where is it set? Can you tell anything about the time of day represented? From what direction does the light come? Where do the shadows fall? How does the painting make you feel?

   • Ask your students to make a copy of the painting. This can be as simple or as complex a process as you are up for. Much can be learned from making a simple pencil sketch. If you are more adventurous, you could use this as an opportunity to introduce your students to different artistic mediums (such as water-color, oils, acrylics, or tempera on plaster - also known as fresco). The projects and media need to be adapted to the ages and interests/abilities of your students, of course.

   • After your students have finished their reproductions of the piece, ask them to talk some more about the original. Do they see new things? Do they understand or interpret anything differently from the way they did earlier in the week?

Chapter 3
Filippo Brunelleschi
1377-1446
and Donatello
1386-1466

Resources:

Famous Men of the Renaissance & Reformation, pages 13-18

Leonardo Da Vinci: Artist, Inventor and Scientist of the Renaissance,
"The Renaissance," pages 10-11
"Perspective," pages 12-13

The Italian Renaissance, pages 10-17

Vocabulary:

export	span	vault
priors	architect	(church) nave (not to be confused with church knave!)
notary	analyze	inclination
apprentice	stunned	crucifix
prominent	transfixed	baptistery
rival	reputation	dimensions
meticulous(ly)	revival	perspective
parallel	converge	horizon
geometry	formulate	commission
scoff	quarry	stucco(es)
cupola		

People and Places:

Florence
Cosimo de' Medici
Donatello

the Middle East
Filippo Brunelleschi
Lorenzo Ghiberti

For Discussion:

1. Locate the city of Florence on a map of Europe or Italy. Describe the growth of Florence. For what things was the city known? Look closely at the map of Florence in the Romei **Leonardo** on pages 8-9.

2. Describe the priors' plans for the new Cathedral. Why did they want to build it?

3. What were some of the more spectacular features planned for the new Cathedral?

4. For what profession was Brunelleschi trained? What kinds of activities did he prefer. What was his father's reaction to his preferences?

5. What was Brunelleschi's relationship with Donatello like? How old were they?

6. For what was the young Donatello known?

7. Study pages 10-11 of the Romei **Leonardo**. Notice the pictures of the two crucifixes mentioned in the Famous Men chapter. Which one do you like better? What about Jesus and his death does each crucifix emphasize? Is one more correct than the other?

8. Look at the two entries in the competition to design the baptistery doors (p. 10 of the Romei **Leonardo**). Which one would you have picked as the winner? Tell why.

9. Why did Brunelleschi and Donatello go to Rome? How did they spend their time there? What did Brunelleschi especially want to learn?

10. Study pages 12-13 of the Romei **Leonardo**. Explain the difference between scientific perspective and a more traditional use of perspective.

11. ***Art Activity:*** Have your students draw the picture on page 12 of the Romei **Leonardo** captioned "And in reality." Help them to see (and apply the fact) that the smaller an object is drawn, the further away it will appear to be.

12. When the officials of Florence called for architects to present their proposals for the completion of the dome, what kinds of suggestions did they receive? How was Filippo's response different from the others? How did he convince the council to award him the commission to build the dome?

13. What was it in Brunelleschi's work that impressed Cosimo de' Medici? It is very worth while to make sure that our students notice that Filippo did not just stop with a good plan - but that he was as meticulous and diligent in the supervision of all the details of carrying out the plan. What kinds of things might that suggest about his character?

14. From the quotation at the conclusion of the chapter, what does the artist and historian Vasari seem to admire most about Brunelleschi? You might have your students write a short essay critiquing Filippo's character. In what ways does he model the Biblical principle, "faithful in little, faithful in much?

Chapter 4

Lorenzo Valla

1407-1457

Resources:

Famous Men of the Renaissance & Reformation, pages 19-20

People and Places:

Byzantine Empire

Vocabulary:

prodigy	complexity	hieroglyphics
persisted	patriarch	prominent
Cardinal	stoic	epicurean
Christian	probabilities	predestination
free will	forgeries	

For Discussion:

1. Why would so many important people be interested in Valla's language skills?

2. In what ways would you expect a Stoic, a Christian, and an Epicurean to differ in their definitions of the True Good? To answer this you may have to do a little research into the basic beliefs of each group.

3. Think of the negative and positive connotations for each of the concepts and synonyms listed below: Which words are positive? Which are negative? Can you think of other characteristics for which there are positive and negative adjectives?

NOT FAT:

skinny	thin
bony	slim
scrawny	lithe

INTELLIGENT:

egg head	smart

GOOD APPETITE:

glutton	hearty eater

For the theologically bold among us: Using **Strong's Concordance** and **Vine's Epository Dictionary of New Testament Words**, do a word study on **predestination, chosen, elect, election, foreknowledge**, and **free will**. Do you agree with Valla's conclusions?

4. What later figures from the Reformation did Valla influence? How?

Chapter 5

Cosimo de' Medici
1389-1464

Resources:

Famous Men of the Renaissance & Reformation, pages 21-26

People and Places:

Gonfaloniere   Medici   Platonic Academy

Vocabulary:

guild   random   ensure

For Discussion:

1. Why did the Medici family have so great an advantage over the other Florentine families?
2. Describe Cosimo's education. What part of his education equipped him for success in his career? What other subjects did he study? How did those affect his activities and interests as an adult?
3. Explain how the "random" selection of the Gonfaloniere was not all that random.
4. In what ways did the Medici come to be influenced by Petrarch and Dante? How did this happen?
5. Discuss the advice Cosimo's father gave him just before his death. Does it appear wise to you? Can you find passages in the book of Proverbs which support or contradict it?
6. How did Cosimo apply his father's advice in his own political career? How well did it work?
7. What was the reason for the Council of Florence? What results were hoped for? What results were achieved?
8. Why did Cosimo ask some of the Greek scholars to remain in Florence after the conference was over? Why do you suppose any of them accepted his offer?
9. What was Cosimo's attitude towards art and artists? What was his relationship with Fra Angelico like?
10. Why did Cosimo have his own cell in the monastery of San Marco? What does this tell you about him? Why did Cosimo want a painting of The Adoration of the Magi painted in his cell?
11. What kind of man was Fra Filippo Lippi? What kind of man was Fra Angelico? What does Cosimo's relationship with each painter tell us about him?
12. Describe Cosimo's relationship with his grandchildren. What conclusions do you draw about his character from this?

Chapter 6

Lorenzo de' Medici
1449-1492

Resources:

Famous Men of the Renaissance & Reformation, pages 27-34

People and Places:

(* indicates a person with their own chapter in *Famous Men of the Renaissance
  & Reformation*)

*Cosimo de' Medici	Piero de' Medici	Lucrezia Tornabuoni
*Lorenzo de' Medici	Giuliano de' Medici	Marsilio Ficino
Pope Sixtus IV	Francesco Salviati	Plato
Girolamo Riario	Francesco Pazzi	Raffaeke Riario
King Louis of France	Pico della Mirandola	Filipino Lippi
Ghirlandaio	*Botticelli	*Leonardo Da Vinci
*Michelangelo Buonarroti	Pisa	Milan
Bologna	Venice	Ferrara
Naples	Rome	Otranto
Careggi		

Vocabulary:

marshal forces	catapulted (to a position)	antiquity
mercenaries	guild	ally
perceive	ambition	annex(ing)
coup	confiscate	indignities
bull of excommunication	defiant	resolutely
declined	squabble	prospect
obstinate	ingratiating	predecessor
cordial		

For Discussion:

1. Describe how the other leading families of Florence reacted to the news of Cosimo's death. How did Piero respond?

2. What were Lorenzo's parents like? Describe his education.

3. Tell about Lorenzo's early diplomatic career. Locate the cities he traveled to on a map.

4. How old was Lorenzo when he took over the leadership of the Medici family? How well was he prepared for the job? How had his father prepared him?

5. How did the enemies of the Medici family respond to the news of Piero's death?

6. Describe how the Pope became involved in the conspiracy against the Medici family. What does this tell you about the state of the church at the time?

7. Who was Francesco Pazzi and what was his dispute with the Medici? What did he hope to gain by joining the conspiracy?

8. What was significant/ironic about the location chosen for the attack on the Medici brothers? How did the people of Florence respond to the attack?

9. Who did Florence hope would aid them in their war against the Pope and the King of Naples? Were their hopes fulfilled?

10. What step did Lorenzo finally take in an attempt to save Florence? What happened in the short term? In the long run? What does his act tell us about his character?

11. What external threat distracted the enemies of the Medici?

12. Once peace was established, what did Lorenzo turn his attention towards?

13. Name some of the people supported and/or influenced by Lorenzo de' Medici. What affect did Lorenzo's patronage and influence have on the reputation of Florence?

14. Why is Lorenzo called "Il Magnifico?" Who gave him this title? Why? Was it deserved?

Chapter 7
Girolamo Savonarola
1452-1498

Resources:

Famous Men of the Renaissance & Reformation, pages 35-38

People and Places:

Lorenzo the Magnificent   Piero de' Medici   Girolamo Savonarola
Ferrara   the Duomo

Vocabulary:

lector   Lenten

For Discussion:

1. How did the leadership of Piero de' Medici compare with that of his father?
2. Describe Savonarola's background. What was the theme of his sermons? Why did people follow him?
3. What was Lorenzo's attitude toward Savonarola? How did Savonarola view Lorenzo? What was Piero's attitude toward Savonarola? How did Savonarola view Piero?
4. Describe Savonarola's "vision" and his interpretation of it. How did the people interpret the "vision?" What event did they associate with the "vision?"
5. How did Piero's flight from Florence give the city into the hands of Savonarola's followers?
6. What was the "Bonfire of the Vanities?" Who participated? Did everyone have the same motivation? How many different reasons can you think of that might have caused a Florentine citizen to participate?
7. How did the Pope respond to Savonarola? How did Savonarola respond to instructions from the Pope?
8. What brought about the sudden change in Savonarola's standing in Florence?
9. The modern tendency is to paint Savonarola as either a persecuted, righteous prophet martyred by a selfish and rebellious people or as a fundamentalist, homophobic, anti-art-and-beauty bigot that we are better off rid of. Adoption of either view alone represents a distortion of the truth. There are both admirable and reprehensible aspects to Savonarola's life and his rule over Florence. An excellent essay assignment for an older student would be to identify what in Savonarola is admirable and worthy of imitation and what is not.

Chapter 8
Sandro Botticelli
1445-1510

Resources:

Famous Men of the Renaissance & Reformation, pages 39-42

Leonardo Da Vinci: Artist, Inventor and Scientist of the Renaissance, pages 26-27

People and Places:

Alessandro Filipepi

Fra Filippo Lippi

Sandro Botticelli

Fra Filippino Lippi

Vocabulary:

resolved

conciliation

For Discussion:

1. How did Alessandro Filipepi become Sandro Botticelli?

2. Tell about Sandro's apprenticeship with Fra Filippo Lippi.

3. Look at Botticelli's and Lippi's Adoration of the Magi, found on page 27 of **Leonardo Da Vinci: Artist, Inventor and Scientist of the Renaissance**. Compare the two paintings by the two different artists (master and pupil). In what ways are the two works similar? In what ways are they different?

4. Describe Botticelli's relationship with the Medici family.

5. Explain how Botticelli came to do paintings with both mythological and Biblical themes.

6. What does it mean to say "wisdom overcomes instinct?" What happens when instinct overcomes wisdom?

7. Do you know of any other significant event which occurred in 1492? (There, now you can report that you've done American history this year as well!)

8. Describe how Botticelli's work changed after 1492. Look carefully at his paintings. How would you describe the changes?

9. How was Botticelli affected by Savonarola? Though we cringe at the thought of such treasures as Botticelli's paintings going up in senseless flames, how might burning some of his paintings have been a good thing for him spiritually?

10. Choose several of Botticelli's paintings, preferably in a full color, large format print. Choose one with a Biblical subject and one with a mythological subject if you can. Choose one that was completed prior to 1492 and one composed later. Study each picture carefully. What do you see? What do the paintings have in common? How are they different? What do you find most striking about Botticelli's work?

Chapter 9
Leonardo da Vinci
1452-1519

Resources:

Famous Men of the Renaissance & Reformation, pages 43-48

The Italian Renaissance, pages 38-41 "Leonardo da Vinci" & "Art & Science"

Leonardo Da Vinci: Artist, Inventor and Scientist of the Renaissance

People and Places:

Cosimo de' Medici	Filippo Brunelleschi	Donatello
Lorenzo Ghiberti	Vinci	

Vocabulary:

illegitimate	prodigy	theorems
lyre	limpid	

Suggestion for Related Science Studies:

As you read about Leonardo's design of machines and his use of gears, you might wish to study how gears work. Several resources are available for such a study. Discovery Toys has several sets of toy gears. Check with your area Discovery Toys representative for information. Delta Science has a kit in its "Science in a Nutshell" series called, "Gear Magic."

Background:

The **Famous Men** chapter on Leonardo covers much of the same information as the Romei **Leonardo**. Much like our earlier study of Giotto, there are two obvious ways to structure this chapter's lesson:

Option One: Have your student read through the **Famous Men** chapter first and get the whole picture. Then have them read (or read aloud to them) the Romei **Leonardo**. If you use the books in this fashion, its probably better to save all of your discussion until the end.

Option Two: Have your students read the **Famous Men** chapter one paragraph at a time, stopping between many of the paragraphs to look at the material covering in the Romei **Leonardo** as it expands and illustrates the material in the **Famous Men** text. The following is a chart giving a suggestion for how to weave the material in the two books together:

Famous Men	Romei **Leonardo**
p. 43, paragraph 1	pp. 6-7, Vinci
p. 43, paragraph 2	pp. 8-9, Florence
p. 44, paragraph 1	pp. 10-11, The Renaissance

Whichever option you choose to follow, please take time to carefully study the paintings contained in the Romei *Leonardo*. The text provides quite a bit of information about the composition of the paintings and how differences in composition change everything about how a painting is interpreted. You should also carefully note Leonardo's use of color, light, and perspective. Though younger students may make simple observations, and you will expect more sophisticated types of analysis from older students, don't underestimate the shorter guys. They have a tendency to surprise us! We can teach them the sophisticated vocabularies. Introducing them to the great masters is part of what is involved in "training their palettes" for quality.

For Discussion:

1. As you ask your students to tell you about Leonardo da Vinci's family background, you might challenge them to consider what the world would have lost had he not been born. In our culture, where illegitimate pregnancies so often end in abortion, it is important to remember that there are no accidental people, however inconvenient or inappropriate the circumstances of their births. (It might be useful to take a minute and read carefully through Psalm 139 at this point.) What was Leonardo's emblem and motto? Why would either be appropriate for him given the circumstances of his birth? What do you think **he** meant by the motto?

2. In what ways did Leonardo show himself to be a prodigy?

3. What was Leonardo's father's profession? Though Leonardo's father seemed to have hoped that Leonardo would also join his profession, how did he respond to his son's obvious talent and interest in drawing?

4. Describe Leonardo's apprenticeship in Verrochio's workshop. What types of tasks would have been assigned to him initially? What evidence is there that his master was pleased with his work? Look carefully at the painting, The Baptism of Christ — both the whole and the detail of the angel's head (there is a color version in the Romei **Leonardo** at the top of page 17). As you look at the whole painting, which figure is your eye drawn to first, then second? How might Verrochio have been expected to react to being surpassed by his apprentice? How did he react?

Art Activity: According to the Romei **Leonardo**, Verrochio's training followed " a long-standing Florentine tradition [in which] drawing was given special attention, with the emphasis on accuracy." One of the practice lessons assigned to Florentine apprentices was to draw the folds in a piece of draped cloth. You might have your students also attempt this assignment. Provide good drawing paper and drawing pencils. For a model, you might have them copy the drapery study done by Leonardo shown on page 17 of the Romei **Leonardo**, or arrange a drapery study of your own. In order to do the assignment well, your students will have to pay close attention to how the lines intersect, carefully observing the details of the model before them.

Art Activity: After reading (or reviewing) the Romei **Leonardo**'s spread on anatomy (pp. 36-37), have your students draw their own hand (for the stubborn, insecure, or downright terrified at the thought of having to draw.... have them just draw one finger!). This can be a very useful exercise in accurately observing and recording details.

5. Though it was obvious that Leonardo had surpassed his master (Verrochio), how did his master respond to him? What does his lack of jealousy as well as Leonardo's apparent lack of pride, tell us about the character of each man?

6. Describe Leonardo's work on *The Horse*. Why is the title he gave to the sculpture ironic?

7. Carefully study Leonardo's painting, "The Last Supper." After your students have studied the painting, consider attempting to draw or paint a copy of it.

8. Why was the Duke of Milan amused at Leonardo's treatment of the prior of the monastery? Did Leonardo treat the prior fairly?

9. Carefully study the "Mona Lisa." After your students have carefully observed the painting, have them attempt a copy of it. Who was the painting done for? Who had possession of the painting? What does this suggest about Leonardo's attitude towards his own work?

10. Study carefully the three paintings of the Adoration of the Magi by Leonardo, Botticelli, and Fra Filippo Lippi. Which one do you like the best? What unique details do you notice in each? How are they all alike? How does each artist's use of color make you feel about the event? What might it tell you about each man's personal response to the event depicted?

11. Describe the competition between Leonardo and Michelangelo to paint scenes in the city hall of Florence. Did Leonardo and Michelangelo respect each other? Did they like each other? What did Leonardo plan to paint on his wall? What were the results of his efforts?

12. Why did Leonardo move from Florence to France at the end of his life? How would you describe Leonardo's feelings as he looked back on his life's accomplishments? How would you answer his question, "Tell me if anything at all was done?" What do you think he meant by the question? How would you describe the tone of the question? What does the question tell you about Leonardo's attitude towards his life? How would you assess Leonardo's life? Was he a success or a failure? Why?

Chapter 10
Michelangelo Buonarroti
1475-1564

Resources:

Famous Men of the Renaissance & Reformation, page 49-54

The Italian Renaissance, pages 44-47

People and Places:

Gonfaloniere   Medici   Platonic Academy

Vocabulary:

guild   random   ensure

For Discussion:

1. How was Michelangelo's family background different from that of Leonardo's? Even so, what do they have in common?

2. How did Michelangelo end up in the service of Lorenzo de' Medici? What was his relationship with Lorenzo like?

3. What does the story of the Sleeping Cupid tell you about Michelangelo's talent? About his character?

4. After the fall of Savonarola, what did the leaders of the Florentine Republic ask Michelangelo to do? What did he make for them? In what way does his sculpture symbolize the spirit of the city of Florence?

5. How did Michelangelo come to paint the Sistine Chapel?

Art Activity: Just so your students can get a little taste of what painting the Sistine Chapel would have been like for Michelangelo physically, you might try this assignment: (which was suggested to us by a homeschooling mom in NC — write us and we'll give you full credit in the next printing! Since then we have seen similar suggestions in more than one resource. Great minds, and all that...) Tape several large pieces of art paper (or butcher paper) to the underside of a large kitchen-type table. Have your student(s) lie on their backs and draw a paintable figure on the paper over their heads. Then have them paint the figure. Obviously they will sympathize with Michelangelo's back and arm aches. The full blown "here's paint in yer eye" version of this assignment involves giving the students tempera paint and paint brushes. Let them experience first hand the effects of gravity on liquid paint. The sanitized "your mother is a wimp" version is to give them magic markers and have them "paint" with them. Either version will work and make the point — though bragging rights go to those who use real paint!

6. How did Michelangelo know Pope Leo X? How long had he known him?

7. What were Michelangelo's duties as chief architect of the Vatican?

8. What was the subject of Michelangelo's sculpture, The Deposition? Where did he intend the statue to be displayed? What is significant about the figure of Joseph?

9. What was Michelangelo's reputation in his home town of Florence? How did the city react to news of his death? How did they participate in his funeral?

Chapter 11
Cesare Borgia
1475-1507

Resources:

> **Famous Men of the Renaissance & Reformation,** pages 55-62
>
> **The Italian Renaissance**, pages 26-31, "The Courts of Italy" & "The Courtier"

People and Places:

Cardinal Rodrigo Borgia	Pope Calixtus III (Alfonso Borgia)
Cesare Borgia	Julius Caesar

Vocabulary:

accumulate	celibate	meteoric
vicar	betrothed	cataclysmic
negotiate	precarious	infuriated
hostile	intercept	nominally
incompetent	bungler	hereditary title
contender	scandalized	irony
ironic	strategic	formidable

For Discussion:

1. Describe the general condition of the Church during this time period. What were Church leaders like in general? What did they value? Whose kingdom was their primary concern?

2. What is a Cardinal of the Church? What were/are their duties? What standards of behavior are they supposed to follow?

3. How would you describe Rodrigo Borgia? How well would you say he discharged his duties as a Cardinal? Aside from the obvious immorality of the situation, why else should Rodrigo have not had a mistress? Note: Though it is never a good idea to dwell on immorality, it is important to understand the condition of the Church leadership at this point in our study. Such an understanding helps our children understand the events leading up to the Reformation.

4. What does Rodrigo Borgia's choice of a name for his son tell us about his expectations /plans or hopes for the future?

5. Cesare Borgia demonstrated excellence in what areas? What did he lack? (a warning to us all not to confuse excellence with godliness!)

6. After Pope Innocent VIII died, who became Pope? What name did he take?

7. What provisions did Pope Alexander make for children? What was his grand plan?

8. When King Charles VIII of France invaded Italy, how did Pope Alexander respond? How did Cesare help defeat Charles?

9. What does the following sentence mean?
   He [Cesare] took the measure of the rulers of the Italian cities and long remembered how they reacted to the threat of French troops.
   How might this information prove useful to Cesare?

10. What was revealed during Pope Alexander's military campaign against the Orsini family?

11. When Pope Alexander appointed his sons Cesare to be papal legate and Juan to be Duke of Terracina, why are the Borgia family's enemies outraged (and just a trifle nervous)? Would you say they were just overreacting?

12. Why couldn't the office of Pope be passed from father to son?

13. How did Pope Alexander attempt to bring about the next best thing to a papal dynasty?

14. Follow Cesare's 1494 campaign against the French on a map of Italy. How did Cesare use geography to his advantage? What fundamental geographic flaw caused King Charles' defeat?

15. Describe Cardinal Orsini's attempt to get rid of the Borgias. How successful was he?

16. What finally defeated Pope Alexander? How did Alexander's death affect Cesare's fortunes?

17. Why did Cesare's plans backfire? Why do you think Pope Julius might have decided to betray Cesare instead of making him his own (obviously strong) ally?

18. How did Cesare spend his time in Spain?

19. Given the fate of Cesare's last brother-in-law, why do you think King Jean d'Albret didn't take Cesare back to Queen Isabella himself? Why do you think he agreed to help him at all?

20. What is your bottom-line assessment of the life of Cesare Borgia? Was he a successful politician? A successful military commander? A successful prince? What do you think God's judgment of his life might be? Does he remind you of any political figure from the Old Testament?

Chapter 12
Niccolo Machiavelli
1469-1527

Resources:

Famous Men of the Renaissance & Reformation, pages 63-65

The Italian Renaissance, pages 32-33, "Violence and Intrigue"

The Prince, by Niccolo Machiavelli

People and Places:

Soderini   Cesare Borgia
Pope Julius II   Livy

Vocabulary:

instigation	lieutenants	notary
chancellor	armistice	militia
mercenaries	gullible	hypocrisy

For Discussion:

1. Review the time span covered by Machiavelli's life. Who was the ruler of Florence when he was born? When he died? Who was Pope when he was born? When he died?

2. What was Machiavelli's family background?

3. What position did Machiavelli hold in the government of the Florentine Republic? What were some of his duties?

4. How did Machiavelli first come in contact with Cesare Borgia? What were his impressions of the man? What impressed him the most about Cesare?

5. When the Medici returned to power in Florence, what happened to Machiavelli? Why? How did he spend his time thereafter?

6. Why do you think **The Prince** shocked people? Is it still shocking? What was its main apparent purpose? Who was it addressed to? What later political figures read and studied the book? What contemporary politicians might you suspect of using **The Prince** as their guide book?

7. What are some of the possible interpretations of the book?

High School Students: assign at least selections from **The Prince** for them to read and then come discuss with you. Even with younger students, you might want to read selected passages aloud and then discuss them.

Chapter 13
Leo X (Giovanni de' Medici)
1475-1521

Resources:

Famous Men of the Renaissance & Reformation, pages 66-72

The Italian Renaissance, pages 34-35, "The Papacy;" pages 42-42, "The Roman Renaissance;" pages 54-55, "Religious Upheaval"

People and Places:

Lorenzo the Magnificent	Piero de' Medici
Giuliano de' Medici	Pope Innocent VIII
Holy Roman Emperor Maximillian	Holy Roman Emperor Charles V
Florence	Venice
Bavaria	Brussels
Rouen	Marseilles
Genoa	Bologna
Wittenberg	Worms

Vocabulary:

ecclesiastical	expulsion	banishment
squander	restoration	elevation
balk	canon law	exemplary
consequently	erupted	embarked
strove	escapades	staunch
garrison	climactic	ebb
casualties	constrained	straits
bestow	illegitimacy	lavish
indulgences	corrupt	presumptuous
condescending	erroneous	propositions
citation	impertinent	papal bull

diet (not the one that has to do with not eating...)

For Discussion:

1. What was Lorenzo's assessment of his three sons? How accurate did his assessment turn out to be?

2. How did Piero live up to his father's assessment?

3. What had Giovanni's education prepared him for? What do Lorenzo's efforts on behalf of his son's career in the church tell you about the condition of the church?

4. How old was Giovanni when he received his first church appointment? What was the office of Cardinal supposed to require? Do you see a slight problem here?

5. In spite of the highly political nature of Lorenzo's activity on behalf of Giovanni, what kind of life does he advise his son to lead? How well did Giovanni follow his father's advice?

6. How did new Pope Leo X (formerly known as Giovanni) use his papal authority? What steps did he take to solve his cash flow problems?

7. How did Pope Leo X respond to Martin Luther's theses?

8. What did Pope Leo X hope to accomplish in excommunicating Luther?

9. As we will see in the chapter about Luther, the Diet of Worms has nothing to do with eating worms. Since Worms is a German place name, the "W" is pronounced like a "V". (Now I know that is the correct explanation, but I still suspect that if you dig a little deeper (heh-heh) you'd find that there really is some connection - some vindication of my own personal suspicions about the ingredients in German cuisine. Actually, I think German cuisine is one of the original oxymorons - look up oxymoron and you can check off your grammar lesson for the day.)

Chapter 14
Erasmus
1466-1536

Resources:

Famous Men of the Renaissance & Reformation, pages 73-76

The Man Who Laid the Egg, Louise Vernon - biography of Erasmus intended for 5th -9th graders

The Protestant Reformation, edited by Spitz has two selections by Erasmus from *In Praise of Folly* and *The Enchiridion*

Vocabulary:

illegitimate	irrevocable	ordain
satirical	vulgate	vantage point
escalated	uncompromising	quip
zenith	on behalf of	treatise
assert	concede	

People and Places:

The Netherlands	Paris	Oxford, England
Thomas More	Jerome	Augustine
Basel	Louvain	Freiburg
the Habsburgs		

For Discussion:

1. What would have been lost if Erasmus had not been born? (Hint: Given the circumstances of his birth, would he be likely to be born today?)

2. Describe Erasmus' background and early education. What was he most interested in?

3. Tell about the time Erasmus spent in England. How did he support himself? Who did he meet? Describe the work of the Oxford scholars. What was their goal?

4. Describe Erasmus' new Latin New Testament. How was it different from the Vulgate? In what ways was it used by the reformers? How did Erasmus feel about the way his translation was used?

5. What does the phrase, "Erasmus laid the egg that Luther hatched" mean?

6. Describe Erasmus' relationship with Martin Luther. Did the two men respect each other? Did they like each other?

7. Why do you think Erasmus declined the Pope's invitation to attend the ecumenical council? What does he seem to have wanted to spend his life doing?

8. What kind of person does Erasmus seem to have been?

9. For more insight into Erasmus' character, have your students read some of his writings. The last two and a half pages of *In Praise of Folly* (pages 20-22 in Spitz) have some harsh biting satire as he describes the follies of popes, cardinals, and bishops. For the kinder, gentler Eramus, see his section on "Of the Weapons of Christian Warfare" from *The Enchiridion* on pages 30-33. Do you understand any better why Erasmus was identified with Luther in spite of his own protests? After reading the chapter on Luther it might be profitable to come back to Erasmus and ask how their understanding of the essentials of the Christian faith differed.

An Overview of Reformation Geography

In order to understand the "Famous Men" and events of the Reformation, the student should be familiar with the basic geography of Europe. That means he should be able to locate and identify from memory such important political divisions as England, France, Spain, Italy, and The Holy Roman Empire of the German Nation. All fifteen of the "Famous Men" come from one of these five nations. In addition, to properly appreciate the challenges faced by Charles V, the student should understand the relationship between all of Charles' far-flung possessions and also the threat posed by the Turks, or Ottoman Empire. Finally the student should know the location of the more prominent cities mentioned in the text.

The best way to learn these basic geographic features is for students to complete their own map (you may photocopy as many copies of the blank map on the next page as you need). The student should locate and label the following geographic features:

Spain	Prague	Wittenberg	London
France	Venice	Worms	The Rhine River
England	Milan	Nuremberg	The Danube River
Holy Roman Empire	Florence	Zurich	The Seine River
Scotland	Rome	Geneva	The English Channel
Madrid	Paris	Rome	

After students have completed their own maps, you can test them on their knowledge by giving them a fresh blank map and asking them to label the important political and geographic features from memory.

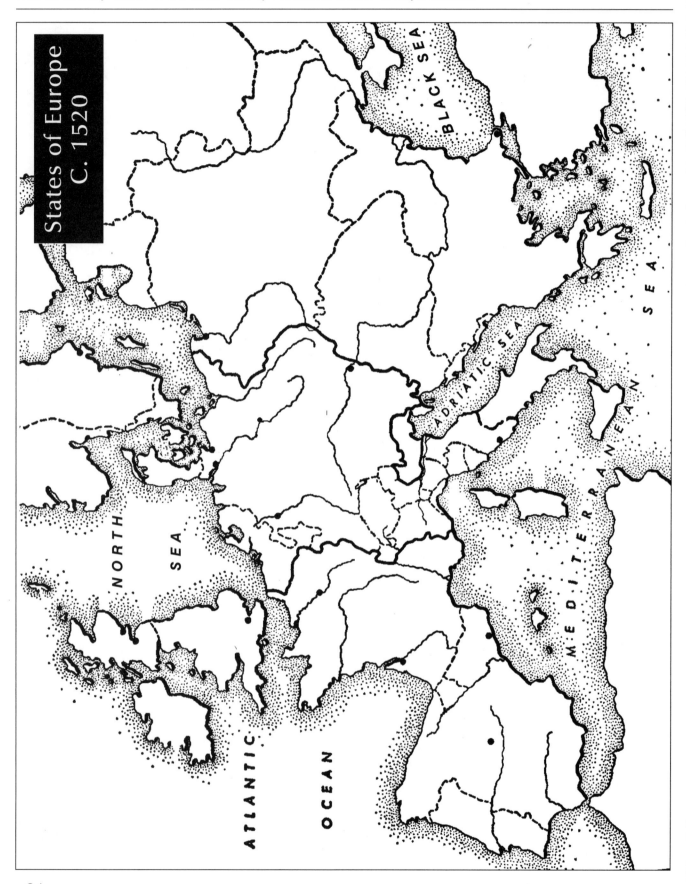

States of Europe
C. 1520

BLACK SEA

ADRIATIC SEA

MEDITERRANEAN SEA

NORTH SEA

ATLANTIC OCEAN

Chapter 15
John Wyclif
1330-1384

Resources:

Famous Men of the Renaissance & Reformation, pages 79-82

The Beggar's Bible, Louis Vernon. Vernon's account of the day Wyclif rose up from what everyone thought was his death bed to give his gloating enemies a tongue-lashing is especially worth reading aloud.

Morning Star of the Reformation

John Wyclif: Morning Star of the Reformation, 60 minute video, excellent, highly recommended

People and Places:

Pope Boniface VIII	King Philip the Fair	Rome
Pope Clement V	Avignon, France	Wyclif-on-Tees
Scotland	England	St. Augustine
Boethius	Chaucer	Oxford
Bruges	Pope Gregory XI	

Vocabulary:

archives	prestige	infamous
corruption	derive	massive
papal bull	regent	schism
transubstantiation	Eucharist	heretical
exile	expulsion	

For Discussion:

1. What were some of the more obvious problems in the practices of the church at the time of John Wyclif?

2. Describe the quarrel between the King of France and the Pope. What was it over? What claims did each one make? What tactics did the King use against the Pope? Who won? How did he win?

3. The 70 years that the Popes were in residence at Avignon has been called the "Babylonian Captivity" of the Church. Why would this be an appropriate name? What was the original Babylonian Captivity and why did it happen?

4. What was Wyclif's educational background? What sort of career do you think he expected to have?

5. What was Wyclif's attitude towards authority in his writings? Who did he believe granted all authority? To whom did he believe all authorities are accountable? How did Wyclif's actions demonstrate that he believed this to be true?

6. Why was Wyclif not arrested when his writings were condemned by the Pope? Who protected him? Why?

7. What did Wyclif believe about the nature of communion?

8. How was Wyclif involved in the Peasant's Revolt of 1381? What ideas in Wyclif's writings seemed to support the peasants?

9. What effect did the expulsion of Wyclif and his followers from Oxford have on the spread of his ideas?

Chapter 16
Jan Hus
1374-1415

Resources:

Famous Men of the Renaissance and Reformation, pages 83-86

John Hus, video

Foxe's Book of Martyrs

Vocabulary:

stir (n.)	emboldened	consecrated
innovations	recalcitrant	excommunicated
safe-conduct	heretic	preliminary
renounce	recant	rector
rally (rallied)		

People and Places:

Prague	Bohemia	Anne of Bohemia
Richard II of England	Jan Hus	John Wyclif
Bethlehem Chapel	Pope Gregory XII	Emperor Sigismund
Council at Constance	Moravian Church	

For Discussion:

1. In the late Middle Ages, what was Prague's reputation? Why did it hold this reputation?
2. What was the first position held by Jan Hus?
3. What connection was there between Hus and Wyclif?
4. Tell about Bethlehem Chapel. Why was it founded? What was unusual about it?
5. How did Hus change the way in which the communion service was typically structured?
6. What items of business were on the agenda for the Council at Constance?
7. What did the delegates to the council want Hus to do? Why didn't they honor the Emperor's safe-conduct promise?
8. Describe Hus' trial. (It is worth reading the "transcript" of the trial from Foxe's. AND it is also worth watching the video...)
9. How could St. Augustine and Paul the Apostle be Hussites?
10. What action did the council take? How did the people of Bohemia react?
11. What church were the followers of Hus associated with?
12. How do the Czech people feel about Hus today? How do you know?

Chapter 17
Martin Luther
1483-1542

Resources:

Famous Men of the Renaissance and Reformation, pages 87-98

Thunderstorm in Church, Louise Vernon - told from the perspective of Luther's son, Hans, who at 12, is trying to discover why his father is so famous.

The Protestant Reformation, edited by Lewis Spitz has four selections by Luther, including the text of the 95 theses.

Vocabulary:

intricacies	vicar	regent
successive	canonical hours	penance
appalled	forum	upstart
critique	adamantly	intimidated
subsequent	salutary	pronouncements
defiance	cloister	private revelation
nunneries	beset	mediate
unblemished reputation		

People and Places:

Mansfeld, Magdeburg, Eisenach, Erfurt (all cities in Germany)

Martin Luther	Corpus Juris	Johannes Staupitz
Wittenburg, Germany	Pope Leo X	Frederick, Elector of Saxony
Augsburg	Cardinal Cajetan	Professor Eck
Leipzig	Emperor Charles V	Diet of Worms
Wartburg Castle	The Knight's War	Katarina von Bora

For Discussion:

1. Why did Luther become a monk instead of a lawyer?

2. Tell about Luther's relationship with Johannes Staupitz.

3. Describe Luther's duties in the Augustinian Monastery.

4. What were indulgences? Why were they being sold? Why was Luther appalled at the practice of selling them?

5. What was Luther's reason for posting the 95 Theses? What did he hope would happen because of them? See pages 42-50 in Spitz for the full text of the theses.

6. What topics other than the sale of indulgences did Luther want to see discussed?

7. How impressed was Leo X with Luther's writing?

8. How did Prierias's treatise change the definition of heresy?

9. What political factors, both within the church and within Germany, protected Luther from arrest and execution?

10. What was the Church's teaching concerning salvation at that time? How was Luther's understanding different?

High School Students: If you have not read Augustine's *Confessions* in earlier studies, read it now to see how Augustine influenced Luther.

11. What country would the Hussite armies have come from? Why would identifying Luther with the Hussites hurt him?

12. Why would Luther agree with his accusers that he was in agreement with a well-known and condemned heretic? How prudent was that? What does Luther's response tell you about his character?

13. How did Luther end up in Wartburg Castle, and how did he spend his time there? Why did he leave?

14. Read the words to *A Mighty Fortress* in the context of Luther's return to Wittenberg in 1522. Do you see new things in them? [We especially like the verse that begins, *That Word above all earthly powers, no thanks to them abideth...*]

15. What demands did the peasants make of the princes? Where did Luther stand in the conflict? What happened to change his mind? What was the result?

16. How did Luther find a wife?

17. Describe Luther's housekeeping strategy (then ask question number sixteen again)! See if your mother will let you apply it to your own house -- a hands-on learning experiment!

18. How did Luther seem to feel about marriage and fatherhood? What do you think life with Luther as your father would have been like?

19. Lest we underestimate the effect of kidney stones and gallstones on a person's disposition, do a little reading on this condition. Hey mom! Now you can say you did science for the day...and reading...and language arts (for practicing alphabetizing skills in looking in and for the encyclopedia)...and math (for finding the page numbers)... have them spell *excruciating pain* (and there's spelling even)! Can you tell the author of the study guide has been having a long day?

20. How much credit did Luther take for bringing about the Reformation of the Church?

Chapter 18
Charles V
1500-1558

Resources:

Famous Men of the Renaissance and Reformation, pages 99-104

The Italian Renaissance, "The Sack of Rome," pages 57-58. There is also a very good map showing the "Lands ruled by Charles V" on the inside front flyleaf.

Vocabulary:

emulate   abdicated   dissident

People and Places:

Charles I   Spain   Holy Roman Empire
Castile   Joanna the Mad   Habsburg-Valois Wars
Charlemagne   Philip Melanchton   Turkey
Saxony

For Discussion:

1. How big was Charlemagne's empire? Julius Caesar's Empire? Charles' Empire?

2. Describe Charles' childhood and education.

3. How well was Charles able to communicate with the different parts of his empire?

4. Who opposed Charles' election as emperor? Who supported him?

5. Who fought in the Habsburg-Valois Wars? Why did they fight? Describe the major battles/events of the war.

6. What prevented Charles from turning his attention to the Lutheran Germans?

7. How did the French aid the Turkish attacks against Charles?

8. Once Charles **was** free to attack the dissident and disobedient princes of Germany, what did he do?

9. Why wasn't Luther's body dug up and burned like Wyclif's?

10. What goal did Charles have for Germany? Did he ever achieve those goals?

11. To whom did Charles abdicate his titles?

Packing Slip

Ship To:	Craig Loo	**Ship From:**	Pilar Stevens
Address:	4346 Avenida Carmel Cypress, CA 90630 United States	**Address:**	20 Fiesta Drive Centereach, NY 11720 United States
Email:	caloo@sbcglobal.net	**Email:**	cstevens@fnol.net
eBay ID:	bookloversusan	**eBay ID:**	retasos2

Transaction ID: 1UX571478C048802B

Item #	Item Title	Qty	Price	Subtotal
6920009094	The Greenleaf Guide Famous Men Renaissance Reformation	1	$5.24 USD	$5.24 USD

Subtotal:	$5.24 USD
Shipping & Handling:	$4.00 USD
Shipping Insurance:	$0.00 USD
Total:	$9.24 USD

This is not a bill.

Note: Thanks for paying with PayPal - the safe way to pay online. It was a pleasure doing business with you.

Chapter 19
Albrecht Dürer
1471-1528

Resources:

Famous Men of the Renaissance & Reformation, pages 105-112

Vocabulary:

goldsmith	diligent	inscription
woodcut illustrations	betrothal	dowry
engravings	foreshortening	the Apocalypse
altarpiece	commissions	protege
pension	coronation	condolence

People and Places:

Nuremberg	Michael Wolgemut	Frankfurt
Mainz	Basel	Aldus Manutius
Maximillian	Bianca Maria Sforza	Milan
Venice	Mantegna	Padua
Willibald Pirckheimer	Frederic the Wise	Charlemagne
Johannes Staupitz	Charles V	Aachen
Antwerp	Cortez	Erasmus
Karlstadt	Melanchthon	

For Discussion:

1. What was Dürer's childhood like? What sort of man was his father? What kind of education/apprenticeship did he receive? When did his talent first become obvious?

2. What parts of Europe did Dürer visit during his youth? Were his journeys typical or unusual for the time?

3. What aspects of Italian art and painting influenced Dürer?

4. Describe the relationship between Dürer and Pirckheimer? What was Pirckheimer's profession? How did he influence Dürer?

5. What type of art did Dürer specialize in? How successful was he?

6. Describe the relationship between Dürer, Pirckheimer and Staupitz. What influence did Staupitz have on Dürer?

7. What did Dürer think of Martin Luther? How do you know?

8. How did Dürer react to the news of Luther's kidnapping?

9. What does the information about the Bible held by St. John in *The Four Holy Men* tell you about Dürer?

Chapter 20
Ulrich Zwingli
1484-1531

Resources:

Famous Men of the Renaissance and Reformation, pages 113-119

The Protestant Reformation, edited by Lewis Spitz includes the text of Zwingli's Sixty-Seven Articles

Vocabulary:

nominally	canton	disputation	dismantle/dismantling
celibacy	monasticism	justification	humanist
escalate(d)	assertion	initiate	militia

People and Places:

Holy Roman Empire	Switzerland	Alps	Basel
Zwingli	Cicero	Zurich	Erasmus
Conrad Gredel	Geneva		

For Discussion:

1. Describe Zwingli's family and educational background.

2. Describe the political make up of Switzerland in 1500. What was their attitude toward the rest of Europe?

3. Why did Zwingli's friends and correspondents refer to him as the "Cicero of our age?"

4. What kind of priest did Zwingli seem to be? How did he spend his time?

5. In what capacity did Zwingli go to Italy?

6. How did Zwingli come to Zurich? What charges did his opponents make against him? How did he respond?

7. How were Zwingli's sermons different from the sermons other priests preached? What effect did his sermons have?

8. What did Zwingli preach about the Scriptures? How did the town council respond? What was the reason for the tension between them?

9. How did Zwingli propose that they settle their disagreements?

10. What were the Sixty-Seven Articles? What was the outcome of the first Disputation? Why was there a second Disputation, and what was its outcome? For the text of the Sixty-Seven Articles, see Spitz, page 82-88. As you read them, notice how often Zwingli makes appeal to the plain teaching of the Scriptures.

11. What does the Doctrine of Transubstantiation teach? What did Zwingli teach concerning this doctrine?

12. What other accepted practices did Zwingli challenge?

13. Who were the Anabaptists? How did Zwingli influence them initially? How did Zwingli feel about the things they taught? What is ironic about Zwingli's opposition to them?

14. What did Luther and Zwingli have in common? Where did they differ?

15. How did the Catholic cantons respond to the Zwingli's reforms? What arrangements were eventually made?

16. Analyze Zwingli's character. In what ways did he behave admirably? In what areas did he not?

Chapter 21
Thomas Müntzer
1488-1525

Resources:

Famous Men of the Renaissance and Reformation, pages 121-124

Vocabulary:

nunnery	convent	exploitation
manifesto	perversion	suppression
opulent	the elect	liturgy
advocate	heretical	assert(ed)
dissolve	advocating	banish
mustered their troops	parley	volley

People and Places:

Thomas Müntzer	Leipzig	Martin Luther
Saxony	Duke John of Saxony	John Frederick
Allstedt	Hesse	Landgrave Philipp of Hesse
Henry Pfeiffer	Muhlhausen	Homburg
Christian League		

For Discussion:

1. Describe Müntzer's educational background. What could such a background have prepared him for?

2. What positions had Müntzer held in the church before coming to Zwickau?

3. Why did the town council of Zwickau expel Müntzer?

4. Tell about the *Prague Manifesto*. Who authored it, where was it posted, and what did the author hope to accomplish by it?

5. What elements of the Prague Manifesto had some Scriptural basis? What elements did not?

6. In what ways might Müntzer have been seen as an ally of Luther?

7. What signs were there that Müntzer was going further than Luther had been interested in going?

8. Describe Müntzer's attitude toward political authorities. Pretend that you are a member of Müntzer's church. You, like Luther and Zwingli, believe that Scripture is the sole authority for faith and practice. Like the reformers, you are willing to challenge many generally accepted traditional practices based on your understanding of the Scriptures. What evidence would you see that Müntzer has problems theologically? (Maybe even psychologically?) What would you have done?

9. How did Jesus say his disciples should respond to those who do not believe (the godless)? What did Müntzer propose?

10. What was the Christian League? What did it do? What was the outcome?

11. Do you agree with Luther's assessment of Müntzer?

12. Make a list of truths and errors taught by Müntzer. Support your answers with Scripture.

13. As you read the next chapter about Grebel and Sattler, be thinking how Müntzer is similar and different from them. Can Müntzer really be called an Anabaptist? Why might the Anabaptists be associated with Müntzer? Why do you answer as you do?

Chapter **22**

Conrad Grebel

1498-1526

& Michael Sattler

1490?-1527

Resources:

Famous Men of the Renaissance and Reformation, pages 125-129

I'll See You Again

On Fire for Christ

The Secret Church, Louise Vernon

The Radicals, a video about the life and martyrdom of Michael and Margaretta Sattler. Highly recommended.

The Protestant Reformation, edited by Lewis Spitz has the text of the Schleitheim Confession as well as an account of the trial and martyrdom of Michael Sattler.

Vocabulary:

advocacy	transcript	grievous	eunuch

People and Places:

Rhine	Strasburg	Heidelberg,
Mainz	Cologne	Conrad Grebel
Balthasar Hubmaier	George Blaurock	Michael Sattler
Turkey	Turks	

For Discussion:

1. Where had Grebel studied? What was his relationship with Zwingli like? What did Grebel think about Zwingli's reforms?

2. What was their major disagreement?

3. Here's part of the question I asked you to think about at the end of the last chapter: Because Müntzer's peasant militias were active during this time, Grebel was associated with Müntzer. How were they alike? How were they different?

4. What was the major distinctive of Grebel's followers?

5. Research the arguments for infant baptism and for adult baptism. What are the Biblical arguments for each? Would you agree with Grebel or Zwingli?

6. What happened to Grebel, Mantz and Blaurock?

7. Who was Michael Sattler, and what was his background?

8. Describe his contacts with Müntzer and with the Anabaptists leaders.

9. What was the *Schleitheim Confession of Faith*? The full text is in Spitz, page 89-96. Could Müntzer have signed it? Why or why not? Could you sign it? Why or why not?

10. Watch the video, *The Radicals* or read the account of Sattler's trial in Spitz, pages 97-101 (this is worth reading aloud!). Discuss your response to it. How do you feel about Michael Sattler? How does he compare with Müntzer?

Chapter 23
Melchior Hoffman, Jan Matthys, & Menno Simons
1496-1561

Resources:

Famous Men of the Renaissance and Reformation, pages 131-135

Night Preacher, Louise Vernon — in this biography of Menno Simons, his life is viewed through the eyes of his two children. Simon lived in hiding, moving from place to place — often suddenly — to avoid arrest. Highly recommended.

Vocabulary:

communal	journeyman	furrier
outlandish	vanquish	besieging
polygamy	straits (desperate straits)	millenarians
anarchist	throng	jurisdiction
appalled		

People and Places:

Tyrol, Italy	Moravian Brethren	Jacob Huter
the Hutterites	Melchior Hoffman	Scandinavia
Netherlands	Gideon	Jan Bockelson (Jan of Leiden)
Leiden	Menno Simons	The Book of Fundamentals
Mennonites		

For Discussion:

1. After the deaths of Grebel, Mantz, and Sattler, where did Balthasar Hubmaier go and what did he do?

2. Where did Jan Hut go and what did he teach? How was he received?

3. Describe the development of the Moravian Brethren. Where are their communities found today?

4. On a map, trace the spread of the Anabaptist message.

5. Tell about Melchior Hoffman. What was his background? What did he preach? Who did he claim to be? How was he received? When Hoffman was arrested and imprisoned in Strasburg, how did Bucer say he should be handled?

6. While Hoffman was in prison in Strasburg, describe the activity of his followers in the Netherlands. Who was Jan Matthys, and what did he do?

7. After Jan Matthys was killed, what new teaching did Jan Bockelson add to the mix? What effect did he have on the citizens of Munster? What happened to the Anabaptists who lived there?

8. How did the actions and teachings of Hoffman, Bockelson and Matthys affect those who believed that infants should not be baptized? Read the elements of the Schleitheim Confession again. How did the teachings and actions of these three men compare with the Confession's points? Could they really be considered Anabaptist? Explain.

9. Tell about Menno Simons. What was his background? Whose teaching did he reject? Whose teachings did he embrace? What did he devote his life to?

10. What was **The Book of Fundamentals**?

Chapter 24
Henry VIII
1491-1547

Resources:

Famous Men of the Renaissance and Reformation, pages 137-142

The Protestant Reformation, edited by Lewis Spitz has the text of Henry's Six Articles

Note: The standard little ditty used to help remember the various fates of Henry's wives goes: *Divorced, beheaded, died, divorced, beheaded, survived.*

Vocabulary:

extensively	martial arts	stillborn
renounce	virtual	chancellor
confer	annulment	persisted
lax	appalled	consummated
null and void	courtier	unenviable
adultery	transubstantiation	celibacy
validity	repose	sovereign (n.)

People and Places:

Henry Tudor (Henry VII)	Arthur Tudor	Catherine of Aragon
Charles of Spain	Princess Mary	Princess Elizabeth
Cardinal Wolsey	Pope Clement VII	Sir Thomas More
Anne Boleyn	Archbishop Cranmer	Anne of Cleves
Jane Seymour	Thomas Cromwell	Catherine Howard
The Six Articles	Catherine Parr	

For Discussion:

1. What was Henry VIII's last name? What was Henry VIII's father called? (So it's good training for games of *Trivial Pursuit!*)

2. For what profession was Henry prepared? Why wasn't he groomed to be king? How was it that he did become king?

3. How did eighteen year old Henry come to marry twenty-four year old Catherine?

4. Tell about Henry and Catherine's children. How did Henry see them as indications of God's displeasure? Why did Henry become dissatisfied with their marriage? What did he want to do about it?

5. Who did Henry make responsible for arranging his annulment? Why was it such a complicated task? How successful was he?

6. Henry broke England's connection with the church in Rome, but was Henry a Protestant? Explain your answer.

7. What was the nature of the "argument" that most impressed Pope Clement?

8. Tell about Henry's relationship with and marriage to Anne Boleyn. What children did she have? What happened to her?

9. What was the *Act of Supremacy*? What was its function? What high ranking officials refused to sign? What were the costs of refusing to sign it? See the note at the beginning of the next chapter for more information on Thomas More's side of this controversy.

10. Tell about Jane Seymour. What children did she have? What happened to her?

11. Why was Henry unhappy with Anne of Cleves? Did she give Henry any reason to annul their marriage?

12. Tell about Catherine Howard. What eventually happened to her? Why?

13. Tell about Catherine Parr. What was her background? How old was she?

14. How old was Henry when he married Catherine Parr? Describe their relationship.

15. What were the Six Articles? The text can be found in Spitz, page 162.

16. Tell about Henry's three surviving children. What were their religious leanings?

Chapter 25
Thomas More
1477-1535

Resources:

Famous Men of the Renaissance and Reformation, pages 143-146.

For a more detailed look at Thomas More's side of this controversy, read or watch ***A Man for All Seasons***, by Robert Bolt. You might want to read the play before you view video production. There are at least two video productions of the play. One stars Charleton Heston (the more heroic interpretation), the other stars Paul Scofield (the more existential interpretation). Though there seems to have been more than one side to More's character, the play does celebrate the heroic and the tragic nature of his stand.

Vocabulary:

prestigious	lucrative	eloquent
grounding	epitome	exchequer

People and Places:

Thomas More	Oxford University	St. Augustine

For Discussion:

1. How far back into his past did Thomas More's loyalty to the House of Tudor go?

2. What had the goal of More's education been?

3. Describe the effect Augustine's book, *The City of God* had on More.

4. What happened to More's legal career as he considered taking vows? What brought him to the attention of the king?

5. What brought More into conflict with Henry?

6. How did More respond to the Act of Succession? In what way did More feel that he was caught between two loyalties?

7. What charges were made against More? What defense did he offer?

Read the next chapter on Tyndale to learn more about More's attitude toward church reform.

Chapter 26
William Tyndale
1494-1536

Resources:

Famous Men of the Renaissance and Reformation, pages 147-152

Bible Smuggler, Louise Vernon

William Tyndale (video)

Vocabulary:

notable	plough	anonymous
syntax	embittered	prologue
diplomatic immunity	lure	prearrangement
irony (ironies)	magistrate	Pentateuch
pseudonym	intervening	

People and Places:

Wales	William Tyndale	Gloucestershire (pronounced *Gloss-ter*)
William Latimer	Bishop Tunstall	Platonic Academy in Florence
Henry Monmouth	Cologne	Thomas Hitton
Kent	Antwerp	Stokesly
Henry Phillips	Thomas Cromwell	John Foxe
Foxe's Book of Martyrs	John Rogers	Thomas Matthew

For Discussion:

1. Where did Tyndale first preach?

2. While he was serving as a tutor, what else did he do?

3. In Erasmus' *Manual of the Christian Knight,* what did he say were the Christian Knight's two chief weapons? This section can be found on pages 30-33 of Spitz.

4. How did the local clergy react to Tyndale's preaching? How did Tyndale defend himself?

5. What did Tyndale believe to be the most serious problem faced by the church of his day? How did he hope to remedy this situation?

6. Who was Bishop Tunstall, and what did Tyndale ask of him? How did he respond?

7. How did Tyndale spend his time when he was in Germany? What did he come home with? How was it received? When the finished book finally reached England, how was it received by the people? The church leadership? What would possession of one of Tyndale's Bibles bring a person?

8. What qualities of Tyndale's translation work made it stand out?

9. How did Thomas More react to Tyndale's translation work?

10. Tell about the trial of Thomas Hitton. Describe the difference between Tunstall and Stokesly methods of limiting access to Tyndale's translation work?

11. How did Tyndale feel about the burning of his books?

12. Tell about Tyndale's relationship with Henry Phillips. What did it result in?

13. What factors had protected Wyclif from arrest and execution? What was different in Tyndale's case?

14. Describe Tyndale's activities in jail? Read Foxe's account of Tyndale's life and martyrdom. What were his final words?

15. How was Tyndale's final prayer ultimately answered?

Chapter 27

Thomas Cromwell

1485-1540

& Thomas Cranmer

1489-1556

Resources:

Famous Men of the Renaissance and Reformation, pages 153-158

Foxe's Book of Martyrs

The Protestant Reformation, edited by Lewis Spitz contains Cranmer's Preface to the Bible and also a remarkable confession of faith penned by Lady Jane Grey. penned four days before her execution on the orders of Queen Mary.

For High School Literature Students: The Thomas Wyatt mentioned in this chapter was also a poet. You sometimes find some of his work in high school level literature anthologies of English literature. The first volume of **The Norton Anthology of English Literature** includes some of his poems, particularly, *"They Flee From Me Who Sometimes Did Me Seek."*

Vocabulary:

brewer	arguably	enact
parish	repeal	implement
coup	staunch	recantation
canvass	intrigued	bill of attainder
acce		

People and Places:

John Dudley, Earl of Warwick (Duke of Northumberland)

Thomas Cromwell	Cardinal Wolsey	Henry VIII
Nottinghamshire	Edward VI	Book of Common Prayer
Martin Bucer	Melanchton	Lady Jane Grey
King Philip II	Sir Thomas Wyatt	Latimer
Ridley		

For Discussion:

1. What had Cromwell's relationship with Cardinal Wolsey been?

2. When Wolsey fell from Henry's favor, how was Cromwell's fortune affected? How sympathetic was he to Luther's reforms? What did he do to further similar reforms in England?

3. What mistakes did he make with Henry?

4. Why was Henry opposed to an alliance with Germany?

5. How did Cromwell's enemies take advantage of the situation?

6. What was Thomas Cranmer's background? How did he get Henry's attention? How did Henry's favor disrupt his marriage?

7. What was Cranmer's relationship with Henry like?

8. How did Henry react to accusations of heresy made against Cranmer? Give examples.

9. Discuss Cranmer's work with the English Prayer Book. What was the book used for, and why were his changes so significant?

10. How did Cranmer's duties change after Henry's death?

11. Describe the make up of the council advising Edward VI. In what ways were Protestantism advanced? How did the actual worship experience change for people during this time?

12. Discuss Cranmer's behavior during the Earl of Warwick's coup.

13. What fatal mistake did Warwick (also called Duke of Northumberland) make?

14. Describe the line of succession among Henry's children. After Edward died, who ruled?

15. How was Mary's accession to throne bad news for Cranmer?

16. What effect did Mary's rise to power have on the nation, specifically on the religious life of the English people?

    Read selections from **Foxe's Book of Martyrs** for more detail about what life was like under Bloody Mary. You might do a report on one or two of the figures you read about.

17. Describe Cranmer's trial and execution.

18. As you read the accounts of these men, both in this chapter and in the earlier chapters about Anabaptist martyrs, why do you think these men and women were willing to die rather than change their beliefs? What kinds of things are this important to you? What do you consider important enough to die for?

19. Read *A Certain Communication* by Lady Jane Grey in **The Protestant Reformation**, pages 169-171. Why (and how) does Lady Jane dispute the usefulness of good works with her theological adverary? What does she believe about the necessity of good works for salvation? How well does she seem to have understood Luther's message?

Chapter 28
John Calvin
1509-1564

Resources:

Famous Men of the Renaissance and Reformation, pages 159-169

The River of Grace, by Joyce McPherson, published by Greenleaf Press. A new biography of the life of John Calvin which emphasizes his childhood, youth and conversion.

The Protestant Reformation, edited by Lewis Spitz, has Calvin's own description of his conversion and call to Geneva as well as excerpts from **The Institutes of the Christian Religion**. It also contains excerpts from Castellio's rebuke to Calvin, *Concerning Heretics.*

Vocabulary:

lucrative	quagmire	slackly	milestone
sacraments	implement (v)	expository	
secular	church consistory	brawling	
fornication	colleague	lament	
obliged	respite	notoriously	
posthumously			

People and Places:

The Institutes of Christian Religion

Jean Cauvin	John Calvin	Picardy
Paris	Orleans, France	Nicholas Cop
Basel	Pierre Robert	Duke of Ferrarra
Geneva	Francis I	William Farel
Society of French Refugees	Bullinger	Hugenots
Michael Servetus	Sebastian Castellio	

For Discussion:

1. What career plans did Calvin's father have for his son? How did Calvin's interests lead him in other directions?

2. What do we know about Calvin's conversion?

3. Why did Cop have to flee Paris?

4. What evidence was there of Calvin's decision to stand with the Protestants?

5. How did the followers of the Lutherans attack the Catholic Church? What was Francis I's reaction?

6. Why did Calvin go to Basel? What did he do while he was there?

7. Who were *The Institutes of the Christian Religion* dedicated to? Describe the dedication. What did Calvin want from the king?

8. How were the *Institutes* organized? How was it received?

9. How did Calvin end up in Geneva?

10. What changes had occurred in Geneva since Calvin's last visit?

11. Describe Calvin's and Farel's activity in Geneva?

12. Why were Calvin and Farel exiled from Geneva? Where did Calvin go, and what did he do?

13. Why did Calvin return to Geneva?

14. Describe Calvin's work in Geneva.

15. What was the church consistory? How was it organized? What did it exercise jurisdiction over?

16. How did Calvin come to be considered a leader of the Protestant reform movement?

17. What was the Geneva Academy?

18. Who were the Hugenots?

19. Describe Calvin's relationship with Michael Servetus. Why was he considered a heretic? What happened to Servetus? What did Calvin attempt to do?

20. Describe Sebastian Castellio's, **Concerning Heretics, Whether They Are to Be Persecuted and How They Are to Be Treated**. What was Calvin's response to the work? Excerpts may be found in Spitz, page 106.

21. Discuss Calvin's last words. What do they tell you about the things he valued? How would you evaluate his life?

Chapter 29

John Knox

1514-1572

Resources:

Famous Men of the Renaissance and Reformation, pages 171-175

Vocabulary:

notorious
harlot   regent   reformulate
reformulated   tactically   house arrest
conformity   profound   lairds

People and Places:

John Knox   Edinburgh   George Wishart
Archbishop Cardinal Beaton   Perth   Queen Mary (of England)
Francis II   Lord Darnley   St. Giles
Mary of Guise (Mary Queen of Scots)   James II (later James I of England)

For Discussion:

1. Tell about Knox's conversion. Who influenced him? What scripture was particularly significant to him?

2. When George Wishart came to Haddington, what service did Knox provide him? (A large two-handed Scottish sword is called a claymore.)

3. Why did he eventually send Knox away?

4. Describe Bishop Beaton's reputation. How was Wishart's death avenged?

5. What made Knox change his mind about accepting a preaching post?

6. Why was Knox imprisoned in France? Who helped get him released? What was his relationship with the government of Edward VI? Why would Edward VI be willing to help him?

7. How did Knox end up preaching to an English congregation in Frankfurt, Germany? What issue did they split over?

8. When Knox returned to Scotland in 1555-1556, how did he manage to upset the Catholic bishops so quickly? How did Mary of England and Mary of Guise both manage to shock him? What was the topic of his most notorious tract, published in 1558? How much did its publication do to win the two Marys to his cause? With which groups were each of the Marys affiliated?

9. How did Knox's friends respond to the tract? Why might Knox expect to have trouble with Queen Elizabeth as well (even though she did return England to Protestantism)?

10. What was the relationship between Mary of Guise (Queen of Scots) and the "Lords of the Congregation?"

11. How did Mary become Queen of the Scots? What deal did she make with the "Lords of the Congregation?" As Mary arrived in Edinburgh, how did Knox "welcome" her? How did this first contact affect his relationship with Mary?

12. Describe Mary's relationship with her husband, Henry Stuart, Lord Darnley? What did he suspect her of? How did she respond to his actions? What was Scotland's reaction to these events?

13. By what name was Mary's son known in Scotland? In England?

14. By which religion did Mary agree to raise him? Who was to oversee his upbringing?

15. The long and bloody history of conflict between the British and the Scots began long before John Knox came on the scene, and continued after his death. It is well worth further reading. You might read **The Scottish Chiefs** by Jane Porter. Robert Louis Stevenson's **Kidnapped**, and its sequel **David Balfour** are set in the context of this conflict, though during the Jacobite rebellions of the Scots in the 1700's.

16. Some might argue that England conquered Scotland, but when James VI became England's James I, whom might you say conquered whom?

17. When Mary of Scotland fled Scotland, who gave her refuge? Describe her relationship with Queen Elizabeth? What did Elizabeth eventually do with Mary?

A small but useful research project — How exactly were Elizabeth and Mary related? A good genealogy of the ruling houses of England and Scotland will prove very helpful.

18. What effect did John Knox have on the Church of Scotland? How could one say that his application of the principle of self-governing congregations and system of lay (not professional clergy) representatives affect American political thought?

Research topic: How could the American Revolution be seen as a continuation of the battles between the Scots and the English for Scottish independence?

Summary Questions:

1. How were the Renaissance and Reformation related? How were they alike? In what ways were they different?

2. What parts of Renaissance scholarship did the reformers find particularly useful?

3. Why were the Anabaptists so unpopular and widely persecuted?

Student_____ Date_____

READING ASSIGNMENT CHART

Topic _____

Book Titles:

    (1)_____

    (2)_____

    (3)_____

Date	Book/Chapter	Pages

Copy as many of these as you need as you plan your study.